Voyager Passport D

ISBN 13: 978-1-4168-0456-7
ISBN: 1-4168-0456-0
206391

Printed in the United States of America

12 13 14 15   WEB   9 8 7

17855 Dallas Parkway, Suite 400 • Dallas, Texas 75287 • 1-800-547-6747

Voyager Passport™ D
Table of Contents

Adventure 1
Ticket to Citizenship

Adventure 2
Keep It Moving

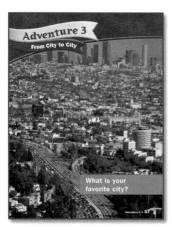

Adventure 3
From City to City

Adventure 4
Reptile Retreats

Adventure 5
Windows into Cultures

Adventure 6
Up Close with Nature

Support Materials

How can you be a good citizen?

Word Works

Word Reading

A

fit	dig	rag	tan
rim	man	sat	mat

Sight Words

B

there	do	other	about
many	some	would	into

Sentence Reading

C

<u>Would</u> you sit on the tan mat?

<u>Do</u> you have to put <u>some</u> bags <u>into</u> the van?

<u>Many</u> of the hats will fit.

One man sat <u>there</u>.

What Is a Citizen?

There are many citizens in a country. They have rights. A baby is a citizen if he or she is born there.

But what if you were not a citizen? You would be **able** to **become** one. This is how you become a citizen.

- Pass a test about the country.
- Say you will do what the **law** says.

I am a citizen. I am glad. I have rights!

Word Works

Word Reading

A

job	hug	box	web
kid	vet	yes	zip
stub	slam	smog	snob
spin	scab	skit	scan

Sight Words

B

each	their	these	people
do	there	other	would

Word Families

C

back	pack	rack	snack
lick	sick	pick	slick
mock	dock	sock	stock
deck	neck	peck	speck

What Does a Citizen Do?

Good citizens have a big job. They **help** other people. They think of all people as equal. That is a big duty.

Citizens can be there for other people. They can make them glad. They can **share** with each other. They can help **Earth**.

You can be a good citizen. Put a box away or take your pet to the vet. Yes, you can be a good citizen!

Word Works

Word Reading

A

with	them	this	path
rush	shut	ship	dish

Sight Words

B

could	was	first	water
been	who	oil	now
each	their	these	like

Sentence Reading

C

Do you see the ship in the <u>water</u>?

<u>Who</u> has a sled with red rims?

I wish I <u>could</u> win <u>first</u> place.

Have you <u>been</u> there?

It <u>was</u> on the top.

Class Rules

Mr. Thash,

   We have many rules in this class. We share, we stop to put trash in the can, and we do not rush or skip in the halls.

   I wish that we could have a **rule** about partners. Some people are not nice when they **choose** partners. It does not **matter** who their partners are. People should be kind to them.

Thank you!
your student,
Seth

Word Works

Word Reading

A

chop	rich	chick	whisk
whip	wreck	knick	knot

Sight Words

B

look	write	number	than
could	people	who	now

Word Families

C

wish	fish	dish	swish
sash	mash	rash	clash
mush	rush	flush	crush

A *Class* Vote

Students can **vote** to choose a class **leader**. Any student who would be glad to help the class could be the class leader.

BALLOT BOX

VOTE

A Good Leader

A class leader must know and do what the students wish. The leader must **plan** to help other people.

Who Wins?

The class must vote in an election to pick a leader. The student with the most votes is the new leader. Can you vote for your class leader?

Adventure Checkpoint

Quick Check

Letter and Sound Identification

A

1. o u e	2. r d n	3. th ch sh
4. n p d	5. i o a	6. o e a
7. th ch sh	8. kn wr sh	9. cl cr ck

Word Reading

B

1. slip ship trip	2. clam clap slam
3. them this then	4. chap shop chip
5. shin then when	6. clip click clot
7. with wit wish	8. mad clad glad

Sight Words

C

_____ there	_____ would	_____ was
_____ many	_____ about	_____ water
_____ who	_____ their	_____ been
_____ do	_____ these	_____ into
_____ some	_____ people	_____ now
_____ other	_____ could	_____ write

Vocabulary Check

Fill in the blank in each sentence with a vocabulary word from the box. Read the new sentences.

plan	share	choose
leader	Earth	rule

1. Will you _____ your food with me?

2. The _____ stood up to talk.

3. Mom will _____ the party.

4. I do not like the _____ about talking.

5. Plants and people live on _____.

6. Which one did you _____?

Word Works

Word Reading

A

feet	needs	weed	seeing
hoop	soon	good	stood

Sight Words

B

come	only	work	years
live	give	our	sentence

Word Building

C

knees	tops	bugs	mats
lifted	cooled	kicked	seeded
looking	asking	doing	handing

My Flag

"What do I need to make a good flag for class?" Neena asked her **grandfather**.

"Have you looked at our flag?" asked Grandfather. "Seeing it can give you **ideas**. It has only three **colors**—red, white, and blue. There are 13 red and white stripes, one for each of the first 13 free states. The stars are for all 50 states."

"Cool!" said Neena. "We have trees on our land. I will add trees to my flag too."

Word Works

Word Reading

A

roads	hood	boats	stay
keep	bay	stoop	jeep

Sight Words

B

over	little	very	after
work	years	live	our

Word Families

C

pay	say	day	stay	play
map	clap	slap	cap	flap

A GOOD LEADER

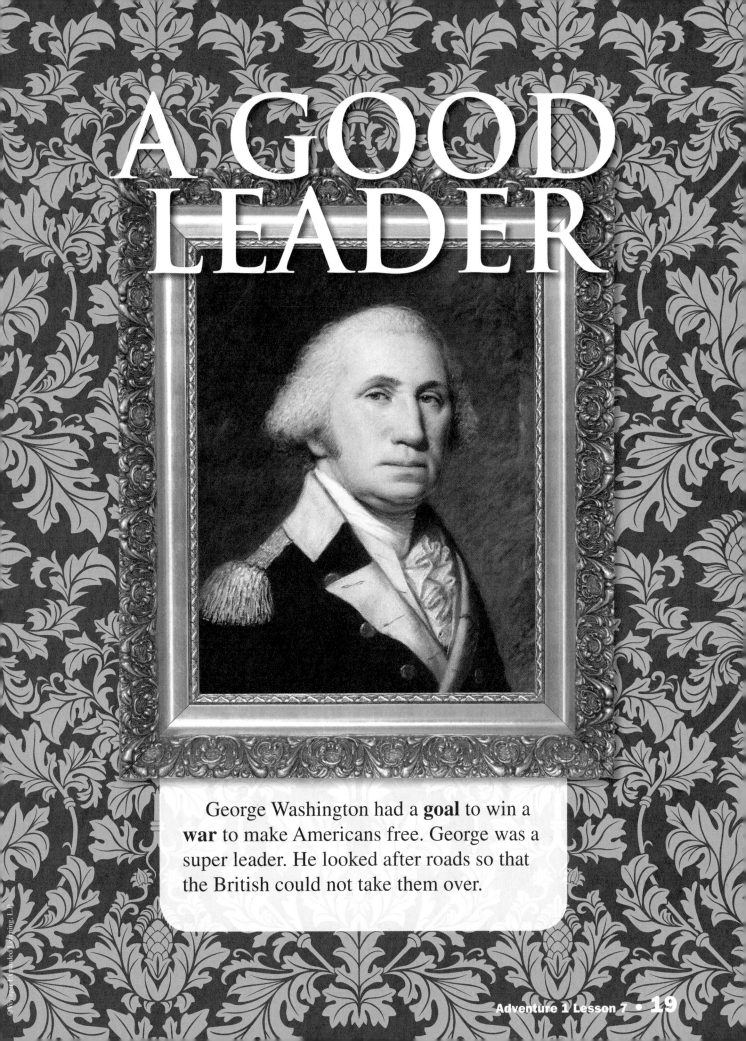

George Washington had a **goal** to win a **war** to make Americans free. George was a super leader. He looked after roads so that the British could not take them over.

George helped find a way to win. He had some men stay on land and other men fill boats on the bay. His plan worked! The British could not win by land or by water.

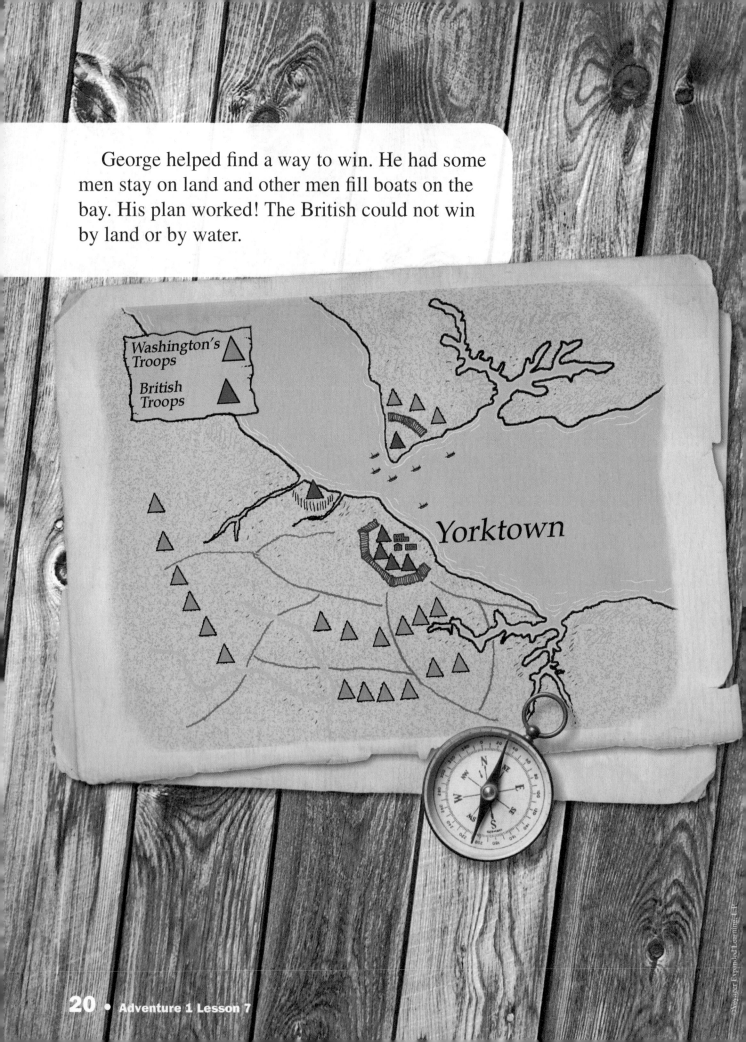

Washington's Troops

British Troops

Yorktown

After the war, Washington **served** as our first president. He made lives better for people.

Word Works

Word Reading

A

always	songs	called	small
sea	reached	malt	bead

Sight Words

B

great	where	through	any
around	does	another	even
over	little	very	after

Sentence Reading

C

I did not see <u>any</u> people there.

A <u>great</u> leader is always calm.

<u>Where</u> did you put my bike?

The heat went <u>through</u> and <u>around</u> the room.

One good team can beat <u>another</u>.

A PROUD SONG

Irving Berlin came to America when he was 5 years old. He was **proud** to be free. Irving wrote many great songs.

His songs reached people all around the **globe** through radio and plays. Over time, Irving became rich. He always gave a lot of his **money** to others.

Irving liked that his songs made people proud of their home. He wrote "God Bless America." In the song, Irving called America his "home sweet home."

Word Works

Word Reading

A

taking	shaking	hoped
used	biting	timed

Sight Words

B

before	right	follow	also
great	where	through	around

Word Families

C

cake	bake	rake	fake	shake
poke	smoke	broke	choke	woke

CLEANING UP

Kate and Pete sat for lunch on the grass. Pete set out white paper plates. Before Kate set a slice of cake on each plate, she saw huge **piles** of litter through the trees.

Pete also saw the piles of paper bags and tin cans. "I do not **understand**," he said. "Why are people not taking their trash to the cans?"

"Come on," said Kate. Kate and Pete **decided** to clean up the piles. They used a bin and recycled the trash.

Adventure Checkpoint

Quick Check

Letter and Sound Identification

A

1. ea oa er	2. ch ck sh	3. tr wr al
4. th ch sh	5. wh wr kn	6. oo ee oa

Word Reading

B

1. wrong long song	2. cot knot slot
3. nest note neat	4. shook ship shape
5. chap chip chalk	6. vote wrote note
7. knife kite life	8. tool tooth tube

Sight Words

C

_____ come	_____ little	_____ any
_____ only	_____ very	_____ does
_____ work	_____ after	_____ another
_____ years	_____ great	_____ around
_____ our	_____ where	
_____ over	_____ through	

How will you "keep it moving"?

Word Works

Word Reading

A

badge	dodge	pledge
edge	lodge	nudge

Sight Words

B

because	again	animal	move
different	air	mother	away

Sentence Reading

C

<u>Move</u> <u>away</u> from the edge of the road.

An <u>animal</u> got into the lodge <u>again</u>.

I have a <u>different</u> badge from you.

The <u>air</u> is cool.

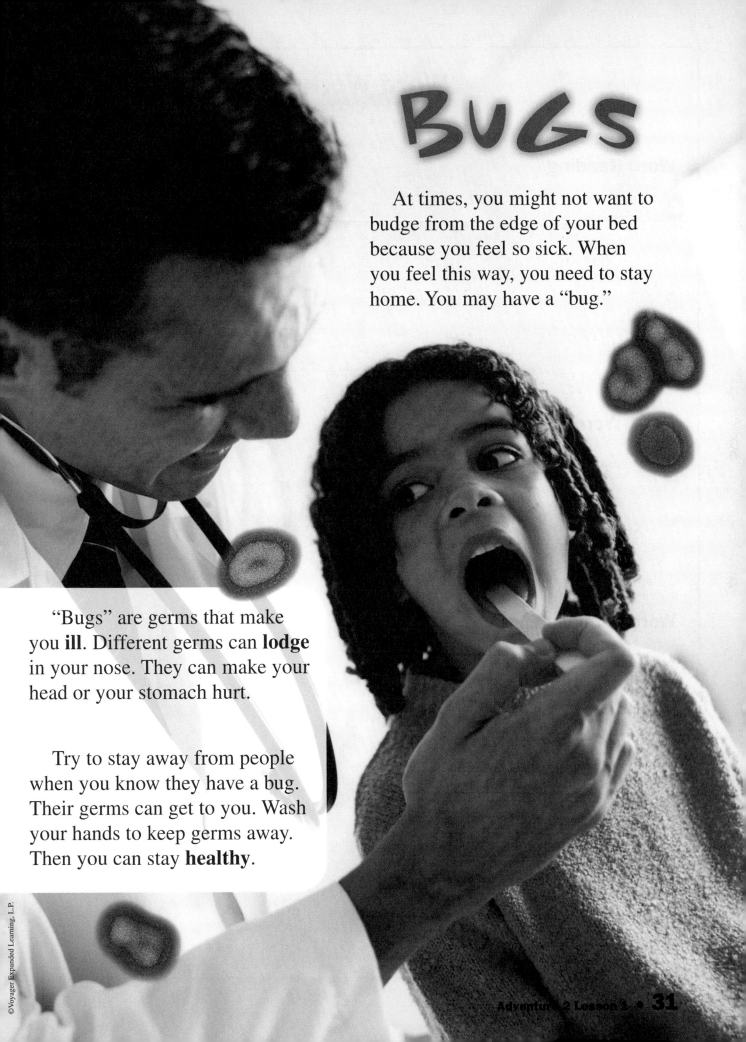

BUGS

At times, you might not want to budge from the edge of your bed because you feel so sick. When you feel this way, you need to stay home. You may have a "bug."

"Bugs" are germs that make you **ill**. Different germs can **lodge** in your nose. They can make your head or your stomach hurt.

Try to stay away from people when you know they have a bug. Their germs can get to you. Wash your hands to keep germs away. Then you can stay **healthy**.

Word Works

Word Reading

A

bake	like	tame	pile
baking	liked	tamed	piling
gem	stage	huge	page
rice	cent	cell	face

Sight Words

B

here	try	picture	letter
different	away	because	air

Word Families

C

well	shell	tell	fell	sell
will	spill	till	mill	bill

Diets for All

Diets are not just for people who want to lose **weight**. It is good for each of us to eat a nice, healthy diet.

©Voyager Expanded Learning, L.P.

Food Groups

Look at the picture. It shows the foods people of all ages should eat. We need to eat a **range** of foods. We do not need too much food.

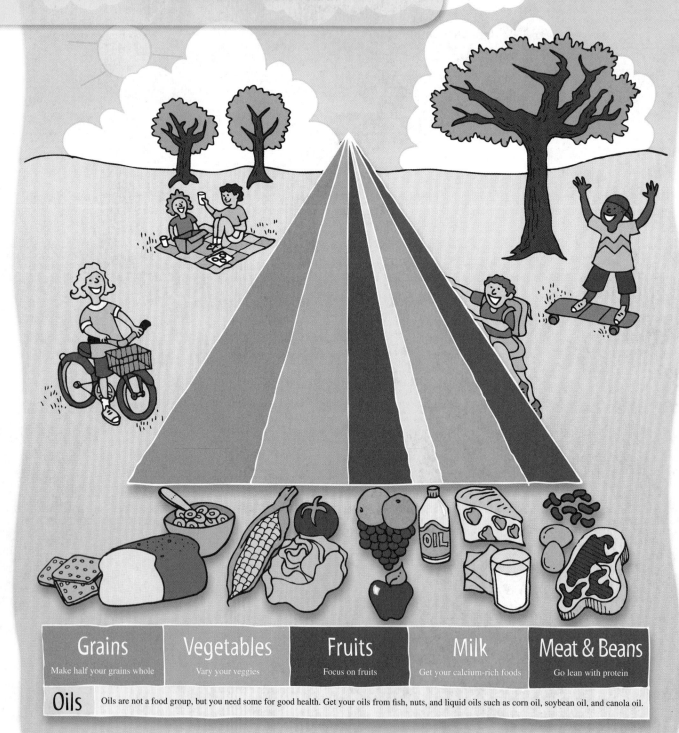

Grains	Vegetables	Fruits	Milk	Meat & Beans
Make half your grains whole	Vary your veggies	Focus on fruits	Get your calcium-rich foods	Go lean with protein

Oils   Oils are not a food group, but you need some for good health. Get your oils from fish, nuts, and liquid oils such as corn oil, soybean oil, and canola oil.

Eating Well

To eat well, we do not have to stop eating foods we like. Just try to make good choices. Snacks do not have to be **fancy**. Fruit or vegetable slices will do.

Total Fat
Saturated Fat 0g
Polyunsaturated Fat 0g
Monounsaturated Fat 0g

Cholesterol 0mg 10%
Sodium 240mg 8%
Potassium 280mg
Total Carbohydrate 43g 14%
    Dietary Fiber 5g 20%
    Sugars 19g
    Other Carbohydrate 19g
Protein 4g

Word Works

Word Reading

A

go	he	she	me
my	shy	fly	by
far	herd	girls	cord
dirt	smart	hurt	form

Sight Words

B

answer	should	world	near
country	father	Earth	eye
different	away	because	picture

Sentence Reading

C

You <u>should</u> sit near me.

My <u>eye</u> hurt when dirt got in it.

The <u>country</u> is on the other side of the world.

To get the <u>answer</u>, you must try hard.

A SPORTS FAN

Marlee knew that she should get more **exercise**, but she did not like **sports**. One day Marlee helped her father in the garden.

Helping Out

Marlee did not think that digging dirt was the answer, but it was! She used all her **might** to dig up the earth and place new plants. She got a lot of exercise.

Shaping Up

Marlee liked this more than jogging in a race. Marlee told Dad that she would start helping him once a week.

Word Works

Word Reading

A

shop	shopping	shopped
nag	nagging	nagged
grin	grinning	grinned
plan	planning	planned

Sight Words

B

learn	every	between	below
should	eye	Earth	near

Word Building

C

jogged	wagging	slapped	hopping
ripping	trapped	pinning	wedded

Sun Safety

Some people like to sit in the sun. Sitting in the sun can give them a suntan. Some people are also letting the sun burn them. They should practice sun **safety**.

Umbrellas can shade your body from the sun.

©Voyager Expanded Learning, L.P.

Too much sun can make you sick. Lotion can keep your skin safe. Learn to wear lotion every day. Do not use a smudge. Take care to use a lot of it. Put more on after each dip in the pool.

Some lotions can help **block** the sun from burning you.

You should keep your eyes safe from the sun, too. Sitting below an umbrella is a good idea. **Harm** from the sun can be stopped.

The sun is strong. It can hurt your eyes.

Adventure Checkpoint

Quick Check
Letter and Sound Identification

A

1. dge st sh	2. r c d	3. th g h
4. ir oi ee	5. ai ar oa	6. or o oi

Word Reading

B

1. huge ham hop	2. star cell slam
3. luck long lodge	4. girls goat gas
5. face fast far	6. brim bridge bread
7. wit sit worn	8. gene seen mean
9. store far mad	10. badge bad mad

Sight Words

C

___ because	___ learn	___ father	___ world
___ air	___ different	___ every	___ Earth
___ here	___ away	___ animal	___ again
___ answer	___ try	___ move	___ letter
___ country	___ should	___ picture	___ eye

Vocabulary Check

Choose the correct word to complete each sentence.

harm	healthy	exercise
weight	might	lodge

1. Write the word that means the damage or hurt that a person feels.

   _____

2. Write the word that means strength. _____

3. Write the word that means feel well or not sick.

   _____

4. Write the word that means to live in. _____

5. Write the word that means things people do to stay healthy or in good shape. _____

6. Write the word that means how heavy something is.

   _____

Choose three words from the box. Use each word in a sentence.

1. _____

   _____

2. _____

   _____

3. _____

   _____

Word Works

Word Reading

A

boy	soy	rain	wait
napkin	canyon	pattern	subject

Sight Words

B

thought	don't	along	something
example	paper	together	group

Sentence Reading

C

The mother gave the boy a <u>paper</u>.

My <u>group</u> likes to play with that toy <u>together</u>.

I rode my bike <u>along</u> the road.

Mary <u>thought</u> she heard a train near the park.

Please <u>don't</u> go too fast.

Pumping Iron

Our muscle groups help us gain strength when we exercise. The main reason to exercise is good health. It can also be something to enjoy.

There are different kinds of muscle groups. Some muscles help you move and **curl** your arms. Other groups of muscles help your heart beat. One group of muscles is used all over your body, even under your hair!

Pumping iron, or lifting weights, is one kind of exercise. You should be careful. This kind of exercise can **strain** your muscles. It can cause **pain**.

Word Works

Word Reading

A

finish	rabbit	puppet
sunset	hummer	river

Sight Words

B

under	story	begin	both	always
don't	group	together	thought	example

Word Families

C

thank	sank	rank	crank	bank
trunk	bunk	chunk	sunk	hunk

Going the Distance

Running is part of a triathlon.

It takes hard work to race in a triathlon. It is a race with three parts. To get ready, racers must work hard at swimming, biking, and running.

Friends Can Help

Friends can help someone **prepare** for a triathlon. They can **encourage** the racer. They can help with training and **practice**.

After the Race

It is good to finish a triathlon. No matter how the race ends, racers can be proud of going the distance. They can also enjoy better health for all their hard work.

Word Works

Word Reading

A

| solo | open | tumor |
| paper | baker | provide |

Sight Words

B

carry	once	hear	idea
enough	really	above	mountain
both	thought	group	don't

Sentence Reading

C

Wearing a tie would be a good <u>idea</u>.

She <u>really</u> likes to play with her dog.

Roy can <u>carry</u> his toys in a bag.

There is more than <u>enough</u> food on this plate.

Put the paper on the shelf <u>above</u> the table.

STRONG TEETH

Growing Teeth

You once had baby teeth. They may be gone now. They may have fallen out so **permanent** teeth could grow. Your teeth grow every day! Strong teeth are **necessary** to chew and swallow your food.

Keeping Teeth Healthy

How can you keep your teeth strong and healthy? Here is an idea: Eat enough of the right foods so that your teeth stay healthy. Eat cheese and yogurt and drink milk. These foods have a lot of calcium, which **strengthens** teeth.

You should also brush your teeth every day. Brushing can keep them clean. Your dentist can show you the best way to brush.

Word Works

Word Reading

A

paper	kidnap	super
hotel	winner	flurry

Sight Words

B

important	children	almost	young
carry	really	idea	enough

Word Families

C

about	trout	stout	without	shout
skin	pin	win	thin	sin

All about Allergies

What Is an Allergy?

An allergy is when your body **reacts** to some things and you get sick. You may sneeze, cough, or get a bumpy, red rash on your skin. You may not breathe well.

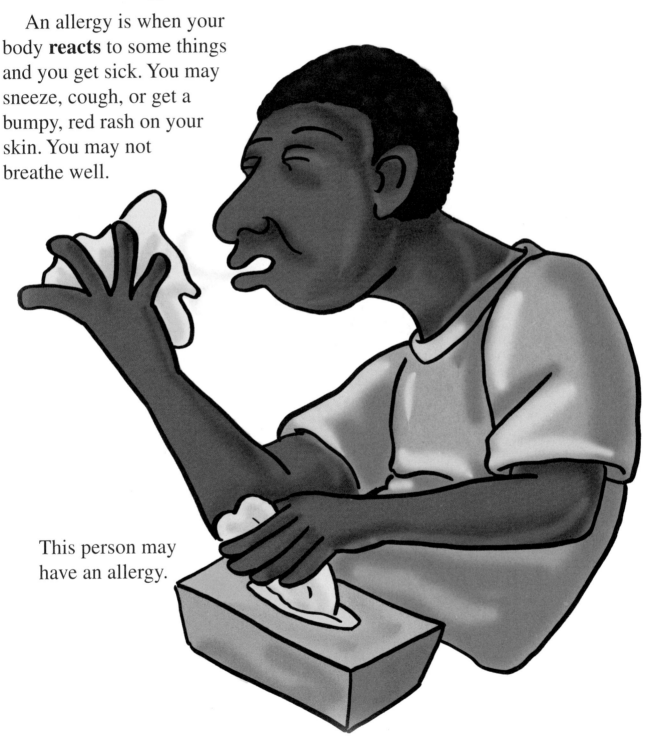

This person may have an allergy.

What Causes Allergies?

Allergies can make people sick.
Some things that cause allergies are . . .

- flowers or other plants.

- foods, like peanuts or milk.

- pet fur.

Flowers like this one can make people sneeze.

Fighting Allergies

People can fight allergies. They should try to **avoid** foods or other things that make them sick. Those who have food allergies should read food **labels**. People can take pills to stop sneezing.

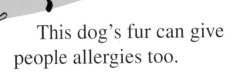

This dog's fur can give people allergies too.

Adventure Checkpoint

Quick Check
Letter and Sound Identification

A

1. oy oa ee	2. y a o
3. ai ea oa	4. ea oo ar
5. oo ee dge	6. d c k
7. l g m	8. e y l

Word Reading

B

1. raid run risk	2. took then toy
3. trip main spin	4. stop star study
5. away play annoy	6. judge hip hug
7. tip train trim	8. my may say

Sight Words

C

___ because	___ something	___ idea
___ thought	___ above	___ carry
___ here	___ mountain	___ again
___ important	___ enough	___ young
___ country	___ really	___ once

What is your favorite city?

Word Works

Word Reading

A

night	bright	sigh
hold	sold	cold

Sight Words

B

family	color	piece
friends	heard	become

Word Building

C

we'll	can't
she'll	I've
haven't	don't

A City Grows

A town is an **area** where people live and work. People might **wander** there if they have heard that there are jobs. Some people might **travel** there to learn.

A town can grow. It can soon become a city. A city can hold many people. It can have many buildings. Some people go to the city to see the bright lights that burn each night. A city can grow again and again.

Word Works

Word Reading

A

how	plow	chow
pie	tie	die

Sight Words

B

sure	door	horse
heard	color	friends

Word Building

C

backpack	everywhere	firsthand
doorman	anyplace	someday

Lucy in New York City

Times Square - 42nd Street

Lucy was glad to be in New York City! The subway was just like she had heard it was. Outside, tall buildings loomed **overhead**.

"Wow," Lucy thought. **Busy** people were moving everywhere in one big crowd. How did so many people fit in one little area?

6609

©Voyager Expanded Learning, L.P.

Lucy walked past many shops. Some shops sold food. Lucy stopped to buy a pie.

There were many lights. There were many other sights! Lucy heard a doorman tell a man on a horse to have a good day! Lucy took a picture of the horse and the doorman.

Lucy was sad when she had to leave. But she grinned when she thought of everything she could tell her friends about her **adventure**.

Word Works

Word Reading

A

begin	window	crazy
because	enters	under

Sight Words

B

today	hours	measure
listen	toward	vowel
door	horse	sure

Sentence Reading

C

Marla and her family moved <u>today</u>.

Last week Jack spent many <u>hours</u> reading under a tree.

The bird moved <u>toward</u> the window.

Amy likes to <u>listen</u> for the bell that rings when class begins.

I need a ruler to <u>measure</u> this stick.

SOUNDS IN THE CITY

"Another morning," says Tim. A truck growls and cuts the **quiet**. Night is ending. From his bed, Tim can listen as his mighty city wakes up. A brown bird chirps. A bell rings as someone enters a pie shop. Car horns now begin to blast.

Tim turns toward the city **noise** of the **early** morning hours. He stands up and looks out of his high window. People start to move around. Tim can hear the voices. Today will be another bold city day.

Word Works

Word Reading

A

sleep	deem	speech
away	play	bay
maid	pain	bail

Sight Words

B

notice	figure	certain
today	hours	toward

Word Building

C

remain	segment	flatten
retire	gutter	unite

Miami: Hot & Cool

Miami, Florida, is a hot spot. Many people fly there on **vacation**. They see the **pretty**, sunny sky. They feel the warm **weather** and the sea breeze. They listen to the waves crash on a sandy beach.

Miami Beach
CITY LIMIT

The city is known for fun. You will notice that there are a lot of things to do. You can shop or try a sport. You can swim and go on a boat ride. You can dance the hours away. You can pet a sea animal! There is no way to measure how much fun you could have!

Miami has a rich past. It was once a Spanish place. Today it is a big, busy port of America. It is full of many different people.

Adventure Checkpoint

Quick Check

Letter and Sound Identification

A

1. ee oo oa	2. oa ay ea	3. ai ea oa
4. e y a	5. ol al oa	6. ee ea igh
7. oa ow ol	8. ie ai ea	9. ea ow oo

Word Reading

B

1. night note neat	2. stay star stick
3. pin pit pie	4. cold coat cop
5. solid sale sold	6. fold fool food
7. stool stain sting	8. brow brim brick
9. fit feet fight	10. drip dries drain
11. try trim trip	12. brook broke boom

Sight Words

C

_____ family	_____ area	_____ hours
_____ friends	_____ become	_____ measure
_____ body	_____ sure	_____ listen
_____ color	_____ piece	_____ toward
_____ heard	_____ today	_____ notice

Vocabulary Check

Each sentence contains an underlined word or phrase that has the same meaning as one of the vocabulary words. Write the correct vocabulary word beside each sentence.

vacation	overhead	quiet	weather
adventure	early	noise	pretty

_____ 1. The flag danced and skipped <u>above the crowd of people</u>.

_____ 2. There was <u>no noise</u> in the room.

_____ 3. The car came <u>before it was time to go</u>.

_____ 4. The <u>loud sound</u> of the cannon shocked the people.

_____ 5. The boy had quite an <u>exciting time</u> at the fair.

Use the three leftover words in the box to complete the following sentences.

1. School was closed because of the stormy _____.

2. The girl with the _____ brown skin wore her hair in braids.

3. This summer, we will take pictures while on _____.

Word Works

Word Reading

A

hound	proud	ground	round
lawn	hawk	shawl	awkward
thief	chief	believe	piece

Sight Words

B

done	English	known

Sentence Reading

C

I believe <u>English</u> became <u>known</u> all over the area.

We were proud when the day was <u>done</u>.

CITY OF ANGELS

Los Angeles is a large city in California. It is often called the City of Angels.

Explorers went to Los Angeles in the 1700s. Railroads reached the city in the 1800s. The people found oil there. **Movies** were made later.

World-Class City

Los Angeles is **famous** for many things. Some are sports and schools. It has important harbors and airports. It is a world-class city.

Hollywood

Los Angeles has lots of smaller cities nearby. One is Hollywood. It has an awesome sign. The pieces of the sign spell the name of the city. Many of the people there are **actors**. Movies are made there.

Word Works

Word Reading

A

below	focus	refer	delight
remake	begin	Friday	recall

Sight Words

B

minutes	front	correct	fact
done	became	known	English

Sentence Reading

C

I will <u>correct</u> the problem.

Joe liked being at the <u>front</u> of the line.

We found a shady place to rest for five <u>minutes</u>.

That is a <u>fact</u>.

I have <u>done</u> all that I can.

SNOOPY'S HOME

Saint Paul is a big city in Minnesota. It is known as the home of Charles Schulz. Charles **created** Peanuts comics. He drew Snoopy, Charlie Brown, Linus, and the rest of the gang for 50 years.

After Charles died, an **artist** made huge **statues** of the Peanuts cast. He sold them to raise money for art schools. Snoopy had a lot of fans! When the sale was done, the schools got a lot of money.

You can go to Saint Paul now to see new bronze statues of Snoopy and his friends. In fact, Saint Paul is still the home of Snoopy.

CANADA

MINNESOTA

NORTH DAKOTA

SOUTH DAKOTA

LAKE SUPERIOR

WISCONSIN

ST. PAUL ⭐

Word Works

Word Reading

A

even	pony	rumor
open	tiger	lazy

Sight Words

B

surface	building	nothing	government
minutes	front	correct	fact

Sentence Reading

C

Our <u>government</u> believes in freedom for all.

There was <u>nothing</u> he could do but sigh and wait.

Notice how smooth the <u>surface</u> is.

Turn right and go to that <u>building</u>.

Music in Memphis

Memphis is a city in Tennessee. If you go to Memphis, **visit** Beale Street. This road is lined with places where you can hear blues **groups** play. These buildings stay open all day.

Plan to visit Graceland. It is clear that there is nothing like it! It was the home of Elvis Presley. Some people call him the king of rock and roll **music**. You can learn about Elvis's life. You can even sign one of the walls!

Word Works

Word Reading

A

weather	bread	heavy	ready
slow	shadow	know	grow

Sight Words

B

course	ocean	scientists
building	nothing	surface

Word Building

C

bowl	thread	shave
frown	cheat	like

SPACE CITY

Houston is near the **south coast** of the United States in Texas. The weather can be hot and damp.

Some people think that only cowboys live in Houston. That is because some people from there like to wear big hats and they like to go see roping shows. There is more to Houston than that.

Some people know Houston for its **space** work. The Johnson Space Center is there. The building was made in 1961.

People can go inside to hear what it is like to go to space. They can feel like a feather as they ride in a fake space ship. It can be a lot of fun. You may grow up and go to space one day!

THE UNIVERSE IS CALLING...

SPACE SHUTTLE

Adventure Checkpoint

Quick Check

Letter and Sound Identification

A

1. ou aw oa	2. ie ai igh	3. ee y ay
4. ur or ar	5. oo ow aw	

Word Reading

B

1. tower snout outer	2. falter folder mailer
3. flip flat flies	4. thing thief thick
5. ship shout shut	6. night knit nip
7. crib crawl cry	8. sheet shield shack
9. acorn away after	10. pilot promise powder
11. claw cling clap	12. super surprise sofa

Sight Words

C

_____ hours	_____ become	_____ today
_____ road	_____ family	_____ area
_____ government	_____ surface	_____ measure
_____ piece	_____ color	_____ listen
_____ done	_____ early	_____ building
_____ English	_____ nothing	_____ friends

What do you know about reptiles?

Word Works

Word Reading

A

insect	river	solid
summer	copy	bobbin
rabbit	model	planet
shiver	medal	habit

Sight Words

B

usually	door	machine
complete	didn't	heard

Sentence Reading

C

We will exit out of the back <u>door</u>.

I will win a medal when I <u>complete</u> the race.

I <u>didn't</u> get to swim in the river.

I <u>usually</u> visit my family in the summer.

Turn the <u>machine</u> on.

Reptile Resting Places

By Michael Zang

Reptiles usually live where it's hot. Many parts of the planet are hot. It sure is hot in the **desert**! Reptiles there like to sleep in the sun. Snakes can nap on warm, solid rocks.

It is hot in the rain **forest** too. Reptiles there have different habits. Lizards can swim in the river. They might get too hot if they don't! **Nature** has many reptile homes. Which place would you like to visit?

Word Works

Word Reading

A

clever	body	shiver
travel	rapid	closet

Sight Words

B

island	though	shown
usually	door	machine

Word Families

C

lean	dean
clean	jean
bean	mean

Cold-Blooded

Reptiles are cold-blooded animals. They cannot turn up the heat, so they must find a way to stay **warm**. They usually sit in the sun and dig under hot sand or mud. It's not easy having cold **blood**!

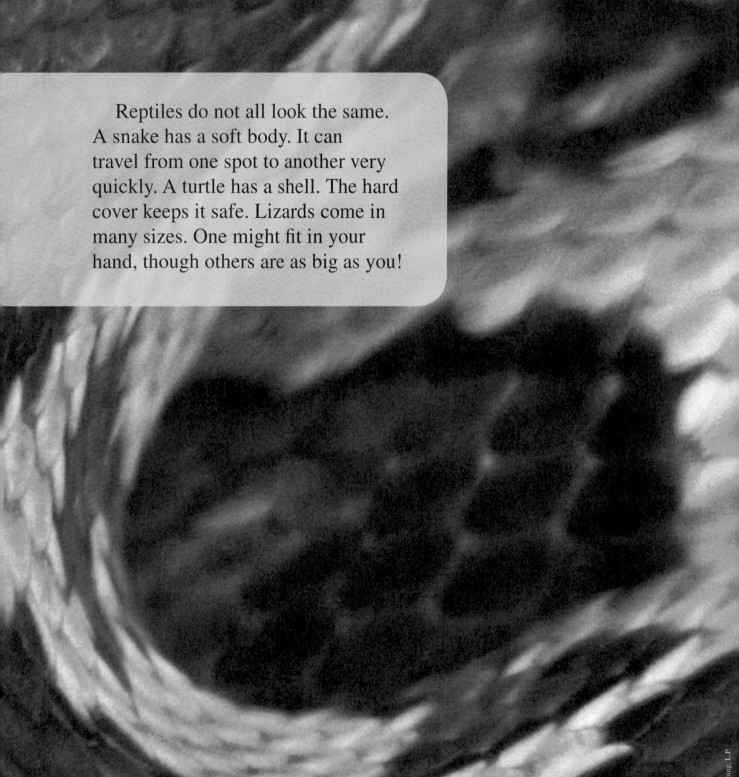

Reptiles do not all look the same. A snake has a soft body. It can travel from one spot to another very quickly. A turtle has a shell. The hard cover keeps it safe. Lizards come in many sizes. One might fit in your hand, though others are as big as you!

Reptiles can do neat things. Usually they lay eggs. They grow a new tooth each time one falls out. Some reptiles can even grow new tails.

Word Works

Word Reading

A

she	go	me	no
my	try	shy	why

Sight Words

B

several	shoe	through
island	though	shown

Sentence Reading

C

It would take <u>several</u> hours to travel to our house.

My <u>shoe</u> tapped to the songs.

I need to get <u>through</u> the gate.

IGUANA DAY

Have you seen iguanas? They may look **lazy**. They can do a lot of things. They can climb and travel.

Iguanas like to eat many plants and certain bugs. They can swim and go **underwater**. They can stay for several **minutes**. Then they have to come up.

These animals are reptiles. They like to sit on the rocks and warm up in the sun. That is a busy day for them!

Word Works

Word Reading

A

pretend	remain	decoy
detain	degree	retreat

Sight Words

B

against	field	travel
several	shoe	through

Word Families

C

feel   peel   kneel   wheel

The Lizard with No Legs

"Lizard!" yelled Gilly Gecko.

"**Liar**, he is a snake!" hissed Sammy Snake.

"What is it?" said Cabot.

"I am certain you are a snake," said Sammy. "You travel like one, and you have no legs."

"He happens to have eyelids and **ears**," said Gilly. "Snakes do not have eyelids or ear openings."

"Do not start a war!" said Cabot. "I am a glass lizard. I never lie. That is important."

"You may be a lizard," said Sammy, "but you are NOT glass!"

"My name comes from my **special** tail," said Cabot. "Pull my tail, and it snaps like glass. I'll get away!"

"Lizards are smart!" said Gilly.

"Snakes are cute!" said Sammy.

"I am the best of both!" said Cabot.

Adventure Checkpoint

Quick Check

Letter and Sound Identification

A

1. ea oa ai	2. oy ai oy	3. ay oa oy
4. oo ol oa	5. ee ea ai	6. ee al ay
7. oa oo ea	8. oy oo ay	

Word Reading

B

1. not neat net	2. cold coat cop
3. lap liar lick	4. incline into input
5. stool stain sting	6. pool pond pose
7. marker mayor meter	8. altar enter eater
9. time tune took	10. team tip tame

Sight Words

C

____ heard	____ door	____ through
____ though	____ island	____ field
____ usually	____ several	____ travel
____ machine	____ shoe	____ against

Vocabulary Check

Choose the correct word for each statement.

lazy	desert	special	warm
ears	forest	minutes	liar

1. I am a place that is dry and hot. _____

2. I stand out from the rest. _____

3. What I say is not true. _____

4. I will not help you work. _____

5. I am home to many trees and animals. _____

6. It takes only a few of these to brush your teeth. _____

7. I have two that let me hear sounds. _____

8. I like sun because it makes me feel this way. _____

Word Works

Word Reading

A

foil	poise	hoist
noise	toilet	soil

Sight Words

B

quickly   stars   pretty

Sentence Reading

C

The box has a very <u>pretty</u> bow on it.

Scientists like to study the <u>stars</u>.

She ran <u>quickly</u> to avoid being late.

One tip is round and one is <u>pointed</u>.

I Think It's a Skink!

By Cora Statler

Do you know what a skink is? It's a **type** of lizard with **shiny** skin like foil.

Skinks like **darkness**. Dark rooms or corners are where you might find them. They move very quickly. If something grabs its tail, the tail will come off and the skink will grow another pointed tail!

If birds fly by, skinks try to avoid being eaten. You might find skinks at rest eating a berry in your front yard.

Word Works

Word Reading

A

new	drew	blew	knew
phone	gopher	graphs	nephew

Sight Words

B

halt	feel	note
quickly	pretty	pointed

Word Building

C

hand	risk	boil
kick	mail	rock

Staying Safe

Do you like snakes? They bring most people to a halt. But how do you think snakes feel? They want to hide from you!

Scientists watch reptiles. They watch what they eat and how they chew. Scientists take notes and draw graphs. They learn how reptiles stay safe.

How can reptiles stay safe? Few move quickly. They cannot fly. Animals like gophers can hide in the ground. Some reptiles can, too. Snakes hide under rocks. The rocks **protect** them.

If a snake cannot hide, it might bite. Some snakes have **poison** in their fangs. Poison can be deadly.

A reptile's color can keep it safe. Some lizards are green, like grass. If a bird flew by, the lizard would be **hidden**. Its color is a camouflage. Some lizards even change colors! Can you see the lizard on this tree?

Word Works

Word Reading

A

fable	little	cable	eagle
pebble	purple	battle	dimple
invite	became	remake	pupil
dislike	explode	include	bacon

Sight Words

B

carefully	contain	course	language
shown	halt	feel	note

Word Building

C

hike	bake	crave
include	fade	slice

SNAKES!

Some snakes will not hurt you. A garter snake is harmless. In warm **seasons**, it **crawls** on the ground. It hunts for little things to eat.

Other snakes are able to hurt you. A king snake uses its strong body to squeeze its prey. It would be a battle to get away. A rattlesnake has teeth that contain poison. A **rattle** on its tail warns others to stay away. If you see one, carefully move away.

Word Works

Word Reading

A

flipping	shipping	skimming
bragged	chugged	fibbed

Sight Words

B

bring	class	stay	strong
course	shown	carefully	contain

Word Building

C

pat	fit	jam
clip	hem	bug

Reptiles as Pets

Do you like pets? Many people have cats or dogs. Some people have pet snakes! Does your classroom contain a pet snake?

Some people think reptiles are pets that don't need much care, stay in one place, and don't make a mess. Those people are mistaken!

Would you like a pet turtle or iguana? Think carefully. A turtle can live for more than 30 years. An iguana can grow to be 6 feet long.

Learn about the reptile you want. Find out how long it lives, how big it gets, what it eats, and what kind of home it needs.

Go to a store to **buy** your pet. Choose a healthy reptile. Be sure it isn't **dangerous** or likely to cause harm. Once you bring your reptile home, you must be **responsible** for it. It's an important chore.

Adventure Checkpoint

Quick Check

Letter and Sound Identification

A

1. ar ai oa	2. oa or oi	3. er ee ea
4. ea ee ew	5. sp ph pr	6. ee ea ur
7. oi oo oa	8. le ol al	9. ar or ir

Word Reading

B

1. norm nose noise	2. chart chat chip
3. poem point phone	4. net nerve never
5. then think thirst	6. topple topping topper
7. praise prize poise	8. hurt hut host
9. fever fewer fester	

Sight Words

C

_____ quickly	_____ certain	_____ shown	_____ fact
_____ front	_____ halt	_____ questions	_____ strong
_____ rest	_____ knew	_____ contain	_____ course
_____ field	_____ feel	_____ bring	_____ language
_____ stars	_____ note	_____ carefully	_____ enough

Adventure 5

Windows into Cultures

What is your favorite holiday?

American Holidays

Holidays are days when we **celebrate** special things. We have many holidays in America. First, we enjoy New Year's Day. It is the first day of the year. Many people sing and cheer as soon as the day starts. In New York, a heavy, bright ball drops. This day is louder than most!

Shortly after New Year's Day, there is Arbor Day. An arbor is a place where we can get shade from a tree. We plant trees on this spring holiday. It is one of the newest holidays. Earth Day is another holiday in spring. We try to show others how to reuse paper and other things **instead** of wasting them.

Next is the Fourth of July. In the summer, we get ready for this holiday. On this day, America became its own nation. We feel prouder about our land on this day. It is common to see fireworks light up the sky.

Last comes Thanksgiving Day. This holiday is **older** than most. Some of the first settlers had to work hard to grow food. Then they had the biggest feast they could. Now some people head home to eat turkey, corn, and bread on this day.

Which holiday do you think is the greatest?

Sequencing

Fill in the chart by writing the holidays you read about in the order in which they appear in the passage. Fill in the season of the holiday, then write about an important part of it.

Holiday	Season	About the Holiday
1.		
2.		
3.		
4.		
5.		

More Holidays!

What other holidays do many Americans celebrate? Name two other holidays and write a sentence about each on the lines below.

1. _____

_____

2. _____

_____

_____

Get Your Kicks

In the 1920s people wanted to get from small farms to big cities. Two men thought that one long road was greatly needed. In 1926, **Route** 66 was born! The road made it speedy to get from Chicago to Los Angeles.

Why Did People Use Route 66?

Route 66 goes through eight states. Farmers used the road to bring food from place to place quickly. Other people moved west to find work.

Shops, gas pumps, and **motels** were added next to the road. People took trips just to drive on the road in their shiny cars. They liked to travel all 2,400 miles!

Where Is Route 66 Now?

You can still ride on parts of the road, but it can be **tricky** to find. Roads were made bigger and better. Hardly any cars were on the first road. Stores closed down.

The road has a long **history**. People still think about how much fun it was to ride on the road. Many know the song "(Get Your Kicks On) Route 66." Will you ride on Route 66?

Vocabulary Practice

Read each line of words. Circle the word that does not mean the same thing.

1. tricky   easy   hard

2. route   path   trip

3. math   history   past

Complete each sentence.

1. It is tricky to _____
   _____.

2. On my route to school, I usually see _____
   _____.

3. I like to learn about the history of _____
   _____.

Adventure Checkpoint

Quick Check

Add -*y* or -*ly* to each word. Say the word aloud to be sure it makes sense.

1. slowly = _____ + ____	2. pick + ____ = _____
3. creepy = _____ + ____	4. loudly = loud + ____
5. shy + ____ = _____	6. soft + ____ = _____
7. sticky = _____ + ____	

Vocabulary Check

holidays	older	route	history
instead	celebrate	tricky	motels

Combine the vocabulary words to make fun phrases. Work with a partner. Match a word with another word on the list to make a phrase. Then, use each phrase in a sentence. Do this two times.

Example: older + route = older route
Route 66 is an older route than many others!

_____ + _____ = _____

_____

_____ + _____ = _____

_____

Comprehension Check

Reread the passage "Get Your Kicks" on page 118. Then complete the activity below.

Read the paragraph. After each sentence, write the question that the sentence answers: *who, what, where, when, why,* or *how*. Some sentences may answer more than one question.

In the 1920s, people wanted to get from small farms to big cities. _____ _____ Two men thought that one long road was greatly needed. _____ _____ In 1926, Route 66 was born! _____ _____ The road made it speedy to get from Chicago to Los Angeles. _____ _____

BOWLING

People from many **countries** go bowling each year. First, you need a bowling ball and a pair of bowling shoes to play. If you do not own these objects, you can rent them at the bowling alley for a low **cost**.

After you have changed into your bowling shoes, you must pay to rent a lane. At the end of the lane are 10 pins. Pins look like bottles. They are lined up to make a **triangle**.

Then you roll a bowling ball down the lane and try to knock down the pins. You play 10 frames, or rounds, in each game. You get two tries rolling the ball in each frame. After each frame, you write your **score**.

You score the most when you knock down all 10 pins with one ball. This special play is called a strike. It is called a spare when you knock down all the pins in two tries. Finally, the player who has knocked the most pins down in 10 frames is the winner, and the game is over.

Vocabulary Practice

Circle the word that means the same as the underlined word in the sentence.

1. The <u>cost</u> was lower because the coat was on sale. (price / free)

2. The <u>score</u> was low for such an exciting game. (points / name)

3. France and the United States are <u>countries</u>. (places / nations)

Write a sentence for each vocabulary word.

1. cost: _____

_____

_____

2. score: _____

_____

_____

3. countries: _____

_____

_____

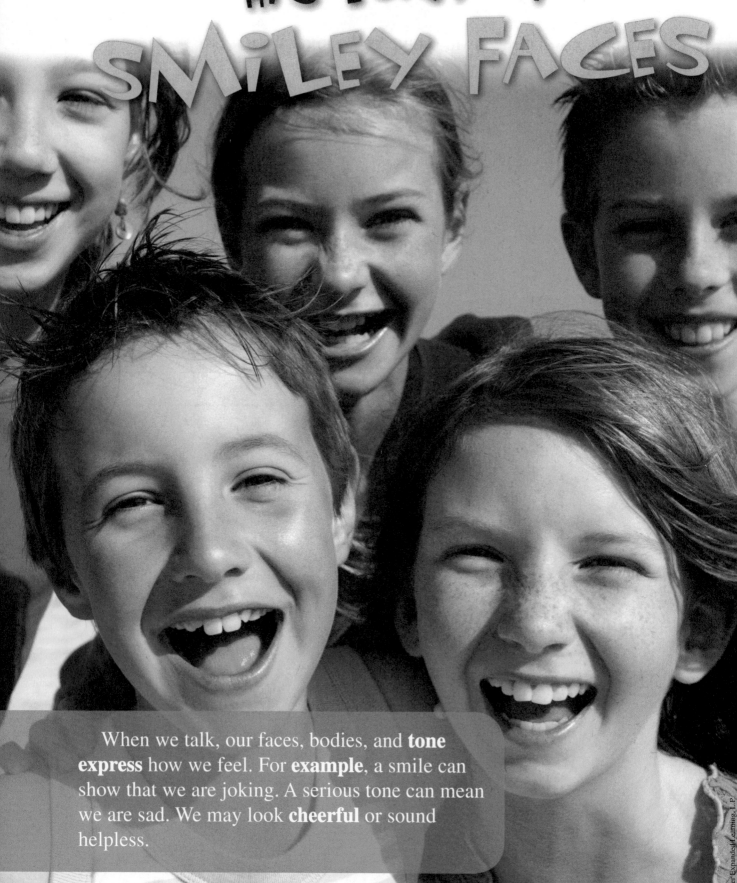

HISTORY OF SMILEY FACES

When we talk, our faces, bodies, and **tone express** how we feel. For **example**, a smile can show that we are joking. A serious tone can mean we are sad. We may look **cheerful** or sound helpless.

©Voyager Expanded Learning, L.P.

In 1982, Internet chat was a new idea. People enjoyed using computers to talk. But they weren't really talking. They were writing. When people wrote, it wasn't always clear how they felt. Someone might write, "Oh great! It's raining." He or she could like rain or be sad it was raining. The reader could not tell just from the words.

Then a man had a helpful idea. First, he used his computer keys to make a smiling face. It looked like this :-). This showed he was joking.

Then he made a frowning face. It looked like this :-(. This stood for sadness.

People found these special symbols helpful. Now they could express their feelings on the Internet. They could tell how other people felt too!

;-)	smile with a wink
:-#	my lips are sealed
:-D	laughing
:-o	surprise
:-O	shock
8-)	smile wearing glasses
:-@	scream

Sequencing

These sentences are from "History of Smiley Faces." Each one has a helpful signal word that tells the order of the details in the passage. Find that word and write it on the line provided:

1. Then a man had a helpful idea.

   Signal word _____

2. First, he used his computer keys to make a smiling face.

   Signal word _____

3. Then he made a frowning face.

   Signal word _____

4. Now they could express their feelings on the Internet.

   Signal word _____

Read each retelling of information from page 129. Put a check mark before the best retelling.

____ Internet chat was new, and people liked talking on computers. But they were really just writing. It wasn't always clear how anyone was really feeling. A person could write about rain without the reader being able to tell how he or she felt about the rain.

____ In 1982, Internet chat was new, and people liked talking on computers. But they were really just writing. It wasn't always clear how anyone was really feeling. A person could write about rain without the reader being able to tell how he or she felt about the rain. Then, a man got the idea to use his computer keys to show a smiling face.

tall tale

Paul Bunyan and his big blue ox, Babe, were strong. Paul was the biggest logger in history. Some loggers tried to work faster, but only Paul and Babe could clear a whole forest in an hour. One day a team worked to build a river dam. A man fell into the water. No one could reach him. The loggers called for help. **62**

Paul Bunyan and Babe were many
states away. Still, the call spread to
them. They knew something serious had
happened. They took a fast route to reach
the calls. Paul looked at the river. He saw
that he must act. Many men were in the
river. They were trying to save the first
man. Instead, they got stuck too. (121)

Paul knew what to do. He waved to his ox, and they got to work. First they bent a hundred trees. Next, they pushed fifty tons of dirt into the river. The river's flow changed. The people were saved. All the workers cheered to express their joy. Paul and Babe were heroes. (173)

Words per Minute _____

Adventure Checkpoint

Comprehension Assessment

Read "Tall Tale" to answer the following questions. Circle the letter of the best answer.

1. Why was Paul Bunyan a hero at the end of the story?

    A. He clears a forest in an hour.

    B. He helps the team finish the dam.

    C. He saves people who are stuck in a river.

    D. He rescues Babe from a falling tree.

2. What did Paul and Babe do right after they bent the trees?

    A. They raced to find the loggers.

    B. They cleared a forest in an hour.

    C. They pushed dirt into the river.

    D. They looked at the river.

3. Where did the story take place?

    A. in a forest

    B. at a beach

    C. at a school

    D. in a desert

4. Which word BEST describes Paul Bunyan?

    A. strong

    B. surprised

    C. friendly

    D. angry

5. What was the main problem in the story?

    A. The river dam was broken.

    B. A logger fell in the river.

    C. Babe got lost in the forest.

    D. Paul was too weak.

Vocabulary Assessment

Circle the letter of the BEST answer to each question.

1. Which word means the same thing as *route*?

   A. path

   B. change

   C. line

   D. pond

2. What is the meaning of the word *express* in the story?

   A. show how you feel

   B. take a break

   C. hide your feelings

   D. feel angry or mad

3. What is the meaning of the word *instead*?

   A. also

   B. in place of

   C. not at all

   D. inside

4. What is the meaning of the word *cost*?

   A. saw

   B. cut

   C. price

   D. swam

5. Which word means the opposite of *older*?

   A. wiser

   B. later

   C. younger

   D. nicer

6. What does the word *history* mean?

   A. later

   B. right now

   C. soon

   D. in the past

In Response

Answer the following question about "Tall Tale" with complete sentences.

What did Paul Bunyan do in the story that real people cannot do?

_____

_____

_____

How do you get up close with nature?

Talking to Animals

Here is a great fact that is **unknown** by many. Animals can talk! They are unable to talk exactly like humans. They talk in their own way. Meet Alex. He is an African Grey parrot. He is very smart. Scientists help him learn new things. Alex can make sounds that are like talking. He knows seven colors. He is learning the alphabet and how to count.

Next, say hello to Koko. She is not a monkey. Koko is a gorilla. She can use sign language to talk. This is a way for her to **communicate**. She knows more than 1,000 signs. That is a lot! She knows many English words. Koko can do almost anything. She is one smart gorilla.

Dolphins can talk too. In general, they are very smart. They have a lot of energy. A dolphin can send a **message** by touch or sound. They may also use eye **contact**. People can shake hands to say hello. Unlike people, dolphins rub fins. All of these skills help them stay alive. Maybe one day, you will talk to an animal!

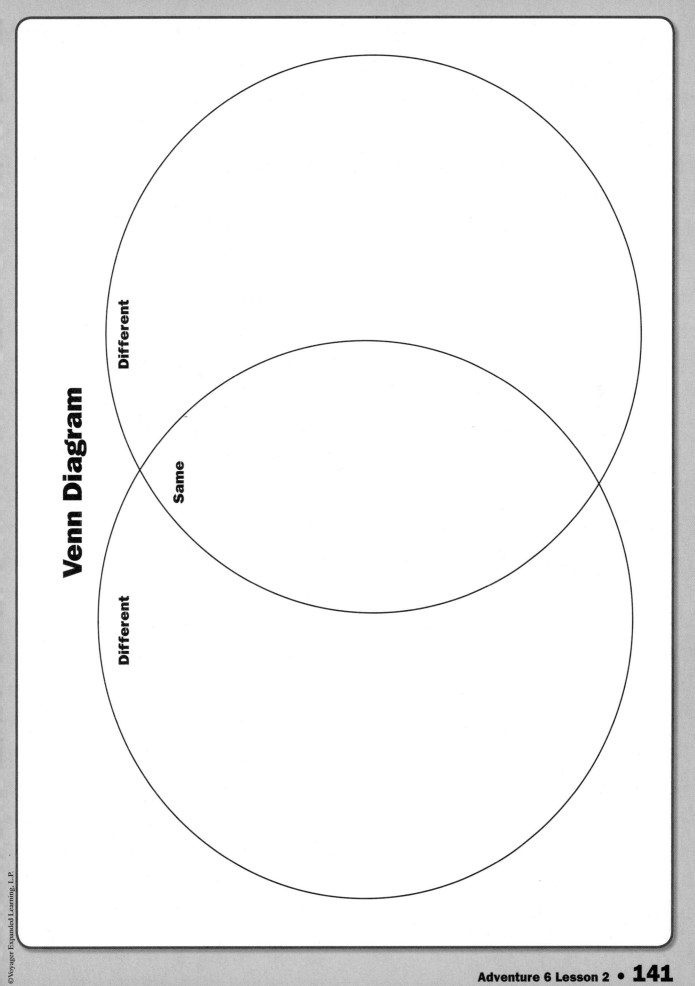

Venn Diagram

Different

Same

Different

DANCE OF THE BEES

By Jin Chung

All of the bees in my family have a job. I have one too. My job is to **search** for flowers. We use the nectar from flowers to produce honey. When I find flowers, I tell the other bees. If you give someone a message, it might be **understood** incorrectly. I make sure that does not happen in our hive!

The other bees watch how I dance. My dance tells them where the nectar is. I have two dances: a circle dance and a waggle dance.

When the nectar is near, I do a circle dance. I turn from left to right. I make an **incomplete** circle. Then I circle the other way. The dance tells everybody that the flowers are near. The other bees fly off to find the nectar.

If the nectar is far, I do a waggle dance. First, I waggle from side to side. Then I run in a straight line. That's how I tell them which **direction** the flowers are in.

I do a perfect job. The other bees collect the nectar and bring it back to the hive. We have enough to make a lot of honey!

Vocabulary Practice

Read each question. Then circle the best answer(s).

1. If you want to be *understood*, what can you do?

    A. talk slowly

    B. moan and cry

    C. ask questions

    D. say hello

2. Which of these words are used to show *direction*?

    A. up

    B. other

    C. few

    D. under

3. Which of these is *incomplete*?

    A. a house with no roof

    B. a girl with no hat

    C. a car with no wheels

    D. a tree with no bird

Main Idea

Follow your teacher's instructions to complete the chart.

Who or What	Important Information	Main Idea Sentence

Adventure Checkpoint

Quick Check

Read the words below. Circle each word that has a prefix.

unkind	friend	different	unknown
sister	incorrect	unlike	after

Vocabulary Check

Match each word with the correct definition. Write the correct letter in each blank.

_____ a note or letter	a. contact
_____ not known	b. message
_____ not finished	c. understood
_____ look for	d. search
_____ knew	e. incomplete
_____ touching	f. unknown

Comprehension Check

Reread "Dance of the Bees." Then, answer the questions below.

1. How is the waggle dance done? _____

_____

_____

_____

2. What does the circle dance tell the other bees? _____

_____

_____

_____

3. Nectar from flowers is used to make _____.

Bugs!

Many insects live right outside your window! Bugs are everywhere. More than a million bugs might live in your own backyard. It might be fun to record the bugs you spot in your yard. Three bugs you might see are a praying mantis, a stick bug, and a dragonfly.

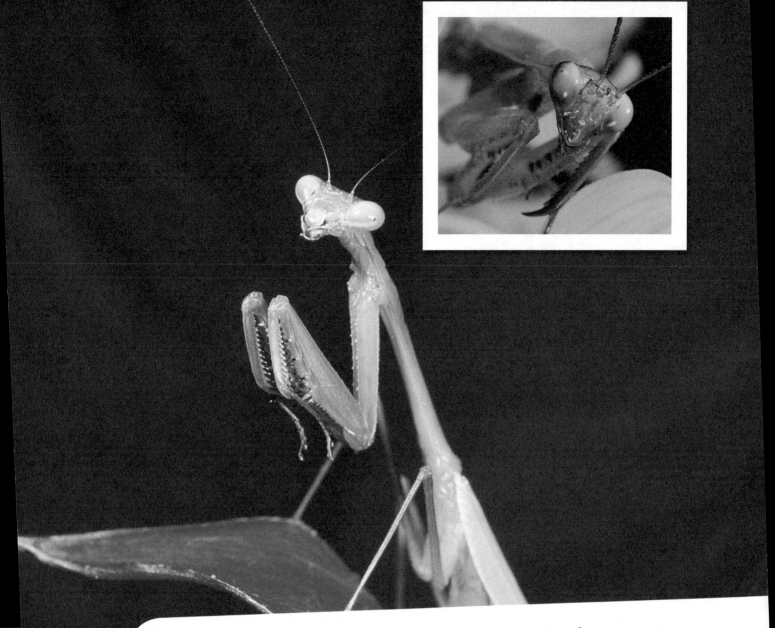

The praying mantis is an interesting bug. It can be green or tan. It likes to eat other insects. Its favorite meal might be a butterfly or a bee. It blends into the plants around it. It likes to **surprise** the bug it will eat. Its two front legs are folded. It looks like it is praying. You will find this bug in meadows. It can turn its head so it can look directly behind itself.

The stick bug is a smelly bug that looks like a stick. It is long and skinny. Sometimes it is called a walking stick. It likes to eat plants. If you **mistreat** a stick bug, it might make a bad smell. Most stick bugs do not have wings.

Lots of people love dragonflies. They are **fascinating**. Their wings seem to **sparkle**. They eat smaller bugs that bite people. A dragonfly can fly fast. More than 5,000 different kinds of these beloved bugs have been discovered.

Check for Understanding

Circle the letter that best fits the statement.

1. This insect can fly very fast.

    A. a stick bug

    B. a dragonfly

    C. a praying mantis

    D. beetle

2. This insect has folded front legs.

    A. a stick bug

    B. a dragonfly

    C. a praying mantis

    D. bumble bee

3. This insect can make a bad smell.

    A. a stick bug

    B. a dragonfly

    C. a praying mantis

    D. bumble bee

Choose the correct word for each sentence or question.

| dragonfly | stick bug | praying mantis |

4. Which insect lives in a meadow?

    _____

5. The _____ has wings that sparkle, and it eats bugs that bite people.

6. You may reach for a stick and find that it is a

    _____.

Lilac Salad

By Marcos Rodriguez

Last night before dinner, Dad threw something purple into the salad. It looked like discolored lettuce. "What is that?" I asked.

"Remember those lilacs we grew in our garden?" Dad tossed the salad, grinning.

"You put flowers in the salad?" I asked, making a face in **disbelief**. "Why did you do that?"

"If you dislike the salad, you don't have to eat it," Dad said. "At least try a bit." He dropped a spoonful on my plate, lilacs and all. "Roses taste good too."

What could I do? I didn't want to treat my dad with any disrespect. I looked around the dining room. My eyes landed on a vase of lilacs on one side of the table. I eyed the salad with distrust, and the tiny purple petals stared back at me. I stabbed some salad with my fork and carefully took a bite.

"Hey!" I said. "This tastes **delicious**!" Suddenly, I thought of an idea. "Next time I see a flower, I will taste it!"

"Hold on," Dad warned quickly. "Some flowers can make you sick."

"What other kinds of flowers are **edible**?" I asked.

"Dandelions and roses taste good," Dad explained. "Even some of those might have **chemicals** on them that can make you sick. Only eat flowers if you know they are safe."

©Voyager Expanded Learning, L.P.

Narrative Text Features

Read the story. Write the names of the characters, the setting, and the plot in the correct parts of the diagram.

Flowers for Grandma

Tim did not know what to do. It was the first day of June, and he did not have a present. It was Grandma's birthday. He loved Grandma and wanted to give her something special. As he walked down the road that afternoon from school, it came to him! He suddenly had an idea for a present. There on the side of the road were the tallest sunflowers he had ever seen. He picked a few and took them home. "Thank you, Tim," Grandma said. "I love the flowers, and I love you."

Story Title

_____

Character(s)

Settings

Important Events

GIANT REDWOODS

Some trees are small, and others are tall. The tallest trees of all are the giant redwoods. These trees grow tall for many reasons. (24)

Some redwoods are 300 feet tall. That is about the same size as the Statue of Liberty. A 6-foot man would look like an ant next to the tree. (54)

The tree has tough bark. It is red and thick. An insect cannot mistreat it. (69)

Giant redwoods grow in a small area. They are found in the western part of America. It rains a lot in this area. The cool, damp air helps redwoods grow. Fog also keeps the trees moist. (105)

Most of the trees are part of a park. No one can cut them. For many, the redwoods are the best part of the park. Everybody likes to look up at the trees in disbelief. (140)

The roots are wide. They can spread far from the base of the tree. This holds the soil in place. (160)

The redwoods are very old. They grow for a long time. Some are 1,000 years old. (176)

The trunk of a redwood has a surprise. It can send a message about the age of the tree. The trunk has rings. Each ring stands for one year. If a tree has 400 rings, it is 400 years old. (216)

Words per Minute _____

Adventure Checkpoint

Comprehension Assessment

Read "Giant Redwoods" to answer the following questions. Circle the letter of the best answer for each question.

1. What is this passage about?

    A. soil

    B. insects

    C. fog

    D. redwoods

2. What is the bark of a redwood like?

    A. The bark is red and thick.

    B. The bark is brown and slimy.

    C. The bark is orange and hard.

    D. The bark is green and moist.

3. What is the last paragraph about?

    A. why the trees need fog

    B. where the trees grow

    C. what the trunk's rings mean

    D. what the tree's bark is like

4. How does the giant redwood compare to other trees?

    A. The redwood is taller.

    B. The redwood is shorter.

    C. The redwood is the same size.

    D. The redwood is found everywhere.

5. What do you think the author wants you to learn about redwoods?

    A. how to save the tree

    B. how to plant the tree

    C. how the tree can grow so tall

    D. how to plan a trip to see the trees

6. Why might a man look like an ant next to the trees?

    A. The trees are much taller than a man.

    B. Ants like the bark of the redwoods.

    C. Ants can grow very large.

    D. Men can grow as tall as a redwood.

Vocabulary Assessment

Circle the letter of the best answer for each question.

1. What means the same thing as *sparkle*?

   A. shine

   B. melt

   C. fade

   D. new

2. If you think something is *delicious*, then you think

   _____

   A. it is large.

   B. it tastes bad.

   C. it is boring.

   D. it tastes good.

3. What does it mean to *mistreat* someone?

   A. You are nice to them.

   B. You are not nice to them.

   C. You shake their hand.

   D. You eat a snack with them.

Use a word from the box to complete each of the sentences below.

message	surprise	disbelief

4. Manny didn't know his aunt was coming to his house. Her visit was a _____.

5. Lily wrote a _____ to her friend on a piece of paper.

6. Rick was in _____ when his team lost the game.

In Response

Answer the question below.

How do the giant redwoods stay moist? _____

_____

_____

Timed Reading Log

	Passage Title	Words Per Minute
1		
2		
3		
4		
5		
6		
7		
8		
9		
10		
11		
12		
13		
14		
15		
16		
17		
18		
19		
20		
21		
22		
23		
24		

Fluency Chart

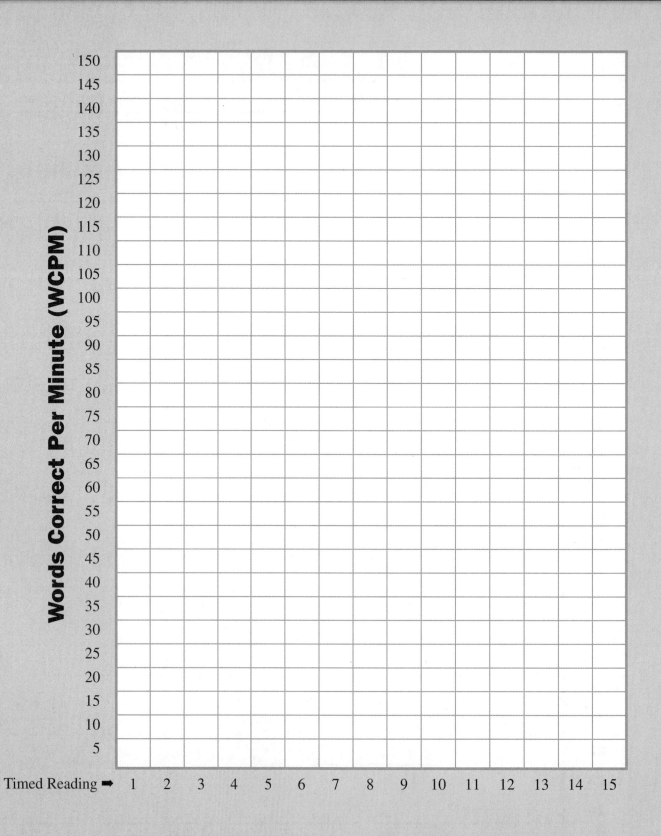

Words Correct Per Minute (WCPM)

150
145
140
135
130
125
120
115
110
105
100
95
90
85
80
75
70
65
60
55
50
45
40
35
30
25
20
15
10
5

Timed Reading ➡   1   2   3   4   5   6   7   8   9   10   11   12   13   14   15

D2

Vocabulary Log

► **Adventure 4**

Vocabulary Log

Vocabulary Log

► **Adventure 6**

Word Families

-ish	-ash	-ush	-ay	-ap
wish fish dish swish	sash mash rash clash	mush rush flush crush	pay say day stay play	clap slap cap flap

-ake	-oke	-ell	-ill	-ank
cake bake rake fake shake	poke smoke broke choke woke	well shell tell fell sell	will spill till mill bill	thank sank rank crank bank

-unk	-out	-in	-ean	-eel
trunk bunk chunk sunk hunk	about trout stout without shout	skin pin win thin sin	lean clean bean dean jean	feel kneel peel wheel

Supplemental Letter Squares

br	pr	gl	sm	s
cr	tr	pl	sp	ed
dr	bl	sl	sn	er
fr	cl	sc	st	est
gr	fl	sk	sw	ing

Who?

What?

When?

Where?

Why?

How?

W

Who or **what** is the paragraph or passage mostly about?

I

What is the most **important information**?

N

What is the main idea in a small **number** of words?

C

Context

P

Parts of Words

R

Resources